A CARE GIVER'S LIFE, LOVE OR OBLIGATION

by Donald Couzens

ISBN-13: 9781234567890
ISBN-10: 1477123456

Cover design by: Art Painter
Library of Congress Control Number: 2018675309
Printed in the United States of America

CONTENTS

INTRODUCTION

The life of a care giver can only be measured by the caregiver's attitude. Are you a caregiver by choice or circumstance? This is the big question you need to ask yourself? If you want to live a good emotional life, this needs to be addressed. If you are sacrificing time to get an "attaboy" or recognition as a martyr, you are heading for disaster. Often, when a person finds themselves in a caregiver role they don't want to be in, they run away to get rid of the situation. If escape is not an option, then this disgruntled individual gets angry or at least, becomes very depressed. Are you finding solace in alcohol or drugs? Are the pressures affecting other relationships pushing you towards divorce, depression, or abandonment? These all can be the end result if you don't take care of yourself. Your health is as important as the person you are helping. If you get sick or are incapable of being there 24/7, it's all over for you and the person requiring care. Even if you are doing this part time because you hire someone to help, or perhaps family members step in to help, it is the same situation to deal with.

There are many issues I will address in this book which I have personally dealt with over the years. Am I suggesting I am an expert on this subject in any way? A big no! Every person caring for someone dealing with Alzheimer's, or any debilitating illness or injury, has their own unique issues. There are no cookie cutter diseases, or injuries, or situations where needs are typical and anticipated depending on where they are in their situation. What one person needs for care is not the same as another person's needs. I will discuss the two situations I have dealt with, however right or wrong. I have lived it and have grown emotionally strong because of this experience. Today, I am a born-again believer in Jesus Christ and can see, in looking back at many of the situations, how God has been walking with me through out my life. God gave me the strength to carry on when I wanted to quit. The bible says in Jeremiah 29:11 *"For I know the plans I have for you, says the Lord. They are plans for good and not for evil, to give you a future and a hope."*

The key in being a gracious caregiver is in learning and developing a spiritual gift called 'patience'. Some bibles call this 'long suffering'. Often times when a need arises and you are asked for something, the first human response is "get it yourself" or "do it yourself". "I am not your slave". If this is you, you cannot be a good caregiver. Was I ever at this point and said such a thing, at least to myself? Yes, I am human and as a young caregiver I was 'put out' to have to provide for someone who gave me life. However, I never verbally responded with this attitude out loud. Was it out of fear or retribution? Who knows? I do remember leaving the room and having ugly thoughts every now and then when I felt overused, not abused. I am an only child who never had to learn to share. My father was my teacher and I saw him sacrifice much for my mother.

Patience is a learned virtue. It is the key to a happy and bountiful life to be able to share with those you love. Galatians 5:22-23 (NLB) *"But when the Holy Spirit controls our lives, He will produce this kind of fruit in us: love, joy, peace, patience, kindness, goodness, faithful-*

ness, [23] *gentleness and self-control;".* Without God in my life, I would not be where I am today. Am I still a sinner, yes, but I am forgiven! Am I still working on having the patience that passes all understanding? Yes. I pray daily and ask God to give me the strength I will need to get through the day and be there for the love of my life.

CHAPTER ONE: A YOUNG CAREGIVER

I feel it is necessary to point out at the outset that I was not saved until I was 38 years old. For those who might not know what this statement means is that I didn't accept the Lord Jesus as the son of God until this point in my life. I know He died on the cross for my sins. It is only through this acceptance that at death I know I will go to heaven to be with Him for eternity.

My mother had an accident where she fell and injured her leg causing many side issues over many years. This situation caused life in our family to drastically change, which I will describe in detail from my perspective. I think my mother frequently prayed to God during this time, but never out loud for me to hear. Children often follow the parent's example when it comes to religion. She frequently quoted the serenity prayer. It says, "God grant me the serenity to accept the things I cannot change, the courage to change the things I can, and the wisdom to know the difference." Today I understand why this meant so much to her.

However, I did not grasp her prayer to God as a young person. I guess I believed there was a God but did not expect anything from Him. I didn't know any different. Walking through the stress of being a young, only child, and caregiver with only societies teachings of what life has to offer, was a real challenge. I was often emotionally mad inside. I had no training on what was required to be a caregiver. I only saw what my father did after he got home from work, but I was never taught the right or wrong way to do things. I am sure my parents did not know in advance I would have to fill this role as caregiver. I was never told anything about the family's financial condition, but money had to be tight because of the medical costs. I can't remember the discussion when I was asked to be the caregiver for my mother during a summer school break when I was 15, but I am sure I felt I didn't have a choice in the matter. It had to be done.

In the 1950's and 1960's life seemed simple as a child, at least until life unexpectantly changed. Wake up, get dressed, go to school, go to bed, repeat. My mother decided we needed to join Indian Guides and my father, and I, were Big and Little Tomahawk. I am sure joining Indian Guides wasn't my idea, but it happened, nonetheless. I remember one interesting project my mother helped me do where we made an album of vacation time pictures pasting them on each page using corner sticky things. We even had a real Indian chief at our house one night for a meeting. Not many other memories of this time. I do however remember being in a kindergarten musical where my mother was prompting me in some song I was trying to sing. I was on stage and she was my prompter. She was able to get around at this point. Then, "It" happened.

We lived in Niles, Michigan on Pokagon Street. This was a small two-bedroom house with a one car garage on the East side. The house was across from the railroad station. My father worked at a factory in town and as I recall, he worked with my grandfather. "It" happened on one fateful day in the early 1950's when my mother decided she wanted something on a high shelf in the kitchen, but she couldn't reach it. Her solution was to get a stool and stand on it to reach whatever it was she wanted. The stool was only three feet tall but given the type of stool it was from this era; it was chrome plated with a one-inch band around the bottom of the legs which gave it the sturdiness this type of stool needed. The seat was padded for comfort and was designed to only be sat upon, not used to stand on to reach things.

Back in the day, a person had to learn to improvise to get things done. Yes, as murphy's law would come into play in this situation, the stool slipped from under her feet and she fell. As she hit the floor, the support band around the stool legs cut and severed her Achilles tendon in her right leg. I must have been in school when the accident occurred because I have no memories of the incident. In fact, I have very few memories of my youth in Niles.

This accident was obviously avoidable had she been more patient, but that is often why accidents are called accidents. I must not have been around much during her recovery because I have no remembrance of her at home and the extra care she would have needed. Where was I? I don't remember if she used a walker, crutches, or a wheelchair. My father was always there to steady her but who helped her when he was at work? I remember spending a lot of time with an Aunt and Uncle who lived in Niles, Michigan, but how did I get to school?

As an only child I felt neglected and did many stupid things to get attention. I was jealous of my friends who had siblings to fight with and share times together. I was jealous because they had parents to do things with. At age 11, we moved to South Bend, Indiana because my father had changed jobs. We first lived in a rental duplex on 29th Street next to the railroad tracks, and then moved to a house on Union Avenue. My mother's leg wound never healed properly and she eventually had to have her leg amputated at the knee because gang green had set in. My father was the care giver my mother needed during the evening hours. During the day, he had a woman come in and cook and care for her while I was in school and he was working.

Someone reading this might say this dialog about my early years is boring and a waste of time to read. I would counter and say our youth years help develop our personality, and how we learn to deal and cope with things today. At the time I felt I suffered a lot and

missed my childhood completely. It clearly wasn't a typical childhood, if there is such a thing. Later the Lord gave me this verse in Jeremiah 29:11-13 (NIV) *11 For I know the plans I have for you," declares the Lord, "plans to prosper you and not to harm you, plans to give you hope and a future. 12 Then you will call on me and come and pray to me, and I will listen to you. 13 You will seek me and find me when you seek me with all your heart.* At the time I did not realize I was in a training class for the future. Does this make all things better, No. I can't erase the thoughts I had back then. With all the COVID -19 lockdown issues being forced on people today, the medical community realizes the youth are drastically impacted because they need interaction with others to fully develop. Suicide and mental illness are a major concern today. Given the restrictions life placed on me, makes me wonder how I survived. When you know and accept Jesus as Lord, things change, and you are mentally and emotionally stronger knowing He is there for you. However, I did not knowingly have this strength in my early years.

Every couple of years my family would take a vacation trip and visit my mother's Aunt in Algonac, Michigan, my Grandfather's sister. On the way we would stop at her cousin's house in Detroit. Even though they were cousins to us, I called them Aunt Lois and Uncle Herb. My parents were close to them especially in their early life together. They had a son; another only child like me. He was like the brother I didn't have. He was 2 years older and doing things I never thought of doing. His parents made him deal with me like a brother and he didn't like it. However, I looked up to him and enjoyed spending time with him, even though it was only for a few weeks in the summer. He had a boat in Algonac, and I loved the water and going out with him for rides.

Going to my Aunt's home in Algonac, Michigan was the high light of my summers when we went. Algonac is a city on Lake St Clair which is really part of the Detroit river. Obviously, it was before my mother lost her leg, but even then, she required assistance in keeping her balance. Waking up in the morning with the windows open and hearing the rumble of the wooden Chris Craft speed boats slowly going down the canal next to the house on their way to open water, is a wonderful memory I will always cherish. When they cleared the canal opening, they hit the power and off they went. The rumble of the Chris Craft engine was awesome. What a pleasant memory and even now I can relive the moment just telling the story. While I was in my own world dreaming about dumb kid things, my father was caring for my mother making sure she had whatever she needed and somehow caring for me too.

While living in South Bend, Indiana, my mothers condition got progressively worse. I was shielded from all of the issues she endured. I don't know how they managed this because it seemed like I was always home.

I do remember their bedroom door was closed a lot, but I never heard any conversations.

After the accident happened and we moved, I remember one time when the Detroit relatives came to visit my parents in South Bend, and they wanted to take me to Detroit with them and live there. Being young and naive, I did not understand why this discussion was taking place, but I was in the house listening to the heated discussion. My parents said no. Later I learned about the addictions my mother was suffering with and why they wanted to help. They were very close at one time and never gave up being there for us. Over the years later they played a major role in my life and gave me some of the parental care I missed at home.

At age 15, I got my first job at the South Bend Country Club as a caddie. This was my first introduction to the world of golf. I immediately fell in love with the game because it was an individual type of sport relying totally on yourself for how you played. I made enough money doing this to pay for a Schwinn bike. I was so proud of this and spent lots of time at the golf course. It was close enough I could ride my bike to get there. This was the perfect sport for me as an only child. It got me out of the house during the summer and therefore, not underfoot. In hindsight, this was selfish on my part, or so I feel today.

Up to this point I did not do much as a caregiver other than cooking. One thing my mother did for me was to teach me how to cook. From her position on the couch in the living room, she would give me instructions on how to fix any dish she wanted for dinner. I had many fun and valued times with my mother as she taught me to cook many of her recipes. Friday night I was responsible for making the popcorn and getting ready to watch the Friday night fights on TV. I wasn't into the boxing, but any reason to eat popcorn worked. I still love popcorn today. On those nights when she wanted beef liver, yuk, my job was to cook the bacon. Yes, I had to eat some liver, but my way, was it took a slice of bacon for every small bite. I really liked bacon, and they wanted me to eat liver. It was a win-win for me, or so I thought at the time. In the early days in South Bend, my father and I would sing together while we washed dishes. It might seem silly to anyone reading this, but you had to be there.

I learned some math skills and logic one summer when my mother was willing to teach me how to play cards. She taught me how to play canasta, Gin Rummy, Cribbage, 500, pinochle, and bridge. It was during these times she had a lot of patience with me, as with cooking. I still cook what we called egg pancakes and enjoy them lots. Not what you would call a healthy meal considering they were eaten with a lot of butter. Yum. Life was not a total bust in my early years but then again, I was in training for the caregiver role even though I didn't know it. As long as I got something out of the effort, I had no complaints. A child's life is basic and simple. This was basic Psychology 101. Make the labor fun and enjoyable and therefore the labor is easy. Little did I know I had started the growing up process sooner than I would have wanted.

During the summer at age 16, I had my first exposure in being a real care giver. At this young age I did not understand all of what my mother had to endure. I later learned she dealt with pain and depression because she no longer could function without help. She became addicted to pain drugs and alcohol. It was very expensive for my father to have a care giver come to the house to be with her when he was working, so during the summer of 1959, I was asked to care for my mother. I thought I knew what was involved but didn't grasp the entirety of the care needed. Providing food for meals was the easy part. It was helping her use the bed pan, cleaning her afterwards, and emptying the bedpan was the hardest. They both smoked and so I got caught up in smoking also. My pay for doing this was a carton of cigarettes when I needed them. However, my mind was not in the effort of being her caregiver. I ended up resenting her more and more each day. When my dad got home from work, I would go out and play with the neighbor kids my age or younger. Life as I knew it, was very lonely.

I couldn't wait to get away when I was old enough. This is hard to say, but at the time my father was my mother's husband, not a father to me. As I said before, I am an only child and I suffered with loneliness and depression. I had moments when I acted out just to get attention, but nothing changed. We did not have a lot of money, but I didn't want for much, except to be loved. It is what we all want. No man is an island.

CHAPTER TWO: ADOLESCENCE CHALLENGES

It wasn't until much later in life when I could face what I had endured as a child and look at what my father did for my mother and appreciate what he taught me through it all. She died at age 50 and I had no feelings of loss when it happened. I was in my early 20's and I felt she took my father from me, and I was mad. I was hurt and found love in all the wrong places. I was sexually active in my teen years and when my girlfriend announced she was pregnant, we married. It was what we were taught to do. Embrace our errors and do the right thing. Later in the year my daughter was born, and it was a hard to imagine I created this living person. Being a parent at age 19 was to say the least, challenging. I didn't know all of what I didn't know at this point in my life. Life's lessons can be hard and cruel if you aren't ready.

I had quit high school to assume the duties of a husband and father. A few years later I did finally finish high school and in 1985 graduated from Eastern Illinois University with a Board of Governors Bachelor of Arts Degree, with an emphasis in Business and Accounting. I got straight A's in _all_ my college classes.

I was even accepted into the University of Phoenix graduate school program and complete two classes with a 4.0 grade point until I had to quit because the money wasn't there to pay for the schooling. This was an accomplishment I could not have done without the support of my wife and the Lord. I can never say it enough. When the Lord is in your life and you are doing what he planned for you, it is amazingly a great experience.

During my younger years I was so naive. In hindsight, I could see how my early role as part time care giver taught me responsibility and how to consider others. My first wife had a promiscuous mother and showed her five children this lifestyle for many years before I came along. She frequently left them alone as she took off for days at a time. As the oldest, my wife had to often care for her siblings. We always lived close so being there for them was never a problem. After we were married, my wife had a job in a diner and worked the midnight shift. I had a job as a home delivery milkman at the time which was good for us. When I went to work there was only an hour when our daughter had to be alone. After I turned twenty-one, I should have suspected something was wrong in our relationship when she would encourage me to go out to the bars and have a good time, whatever that meant. She was pushing me away towards a lifestyle I was not familiar with. My wife's youngest sister had come to live with us at this time, so she was there if our daughter woke up. One fateful morning as I was working my route I came by our apartment and saw a strange car in front. I stopped and found my wife and a strange guy on the couch kissing and petting and I assumed getting ready to have sex. I was mad and broken hearted. Another love shattered. I went into the apartment and told the guy to leave and he did without issue. Because I would never have cheated on my wife, I naively expected her to do the same. Again, I had to face the reality of more growing up. I was angry with my wife, my mother, and life. I had no close friends to lean on for support during this time and thankfully drinking did nothing for me but cause more pain the next day.

I tried to be the husband and father I needed to be, and often made the statement I would be there for my family better than my father was for me. Obviously, I failed but I did the best I could with the training I had at this time. I moved out and within a year my wife moved with my daughter out of state to be with her mother in Arizona. She filed for divorce soon thereafter. I share this story because when we look back at the events in our life and see where we are today compared to where we have been, we can see how these situations form us to be who we are now.

The important detail in this observation is critical in the role of a caregiver. The one trait a caregiver needs, absolutely must have, is patience. As a Christian, there are many gifts of the Spirit we can receive, but in this role it is 'longsuffering', or more commonly referred to as patience as mentioned in the bible. Recently, another caregiver who is helping her husband deal with the disease told me he has called her many names in anger which was so out of character for him. As her tears were flowing as she told me this, you could see and feel she really loves him. Can you turn the other cheek, or do you feel the need to respond? A response in this scenario is counterproductive. The other person has probably already forgotten the incident. But it still hurts.

This reality is based on how we have reacted to get through all of life's lessons in the past. Some lessons we fail to learn, so God gives them to us again. God had given me the strength to walk forward with a positive attitude instead of falling into drugs or booze to hide my loneliness and depression. As an only child, I was being prepared to be alone. Was I happy about this? No, of course not! I was not a recluse, but I could handle being alone if necessary. Most of all, I just wanted to be loved like we all really do.

In 1970 I married my second wife. She was the divorced mother of a young child. Her father owned the property where my employer placed an office trailer. She shared a store with her father and had a clothing boutique while her father sold antiques and was a realtor. He was instrumental in bringing us together because he wanted a father for his grandson, not a husband for his daughter. After a few years I adopted her son and tried to be a good father but always fell short. This was on me. Life together with her was anything but idealistic. I worked for a telecommunications Engineering company and we moved four times before I got a job with the Michigan State Government. Another confession I need to make is the fact I was fired from this job working for the State of Michigan. I was always a great employee and did the job well, but I had lied about having a college degree. It was a requirement for this job. I had the experience and knowledge to do the job but had no degree. I always got good evaluations from the annual reviews. During a highly contested case one year, the truth came out and my employer had no choice but to discharge me. it was the only time I was ever fired from a job. During my few months off I learned to pray to God daily and ask His help in finding a new position. Did I consider myself a born-again believer? At that time, not at all. However, I always felt better sharing my concern with Him and did learn to pray for all needs. I was extremely blessed when a local telephone company hired me. At the time I did not give the Lord credit for this answer to prayer. I did realize I was extremely blessed.

After 10 years of marriage and the recent events of losing a job, I learned she was still madly in love with her high school boy friend who had married someone else. Because of this she could never commit to me. Spousal love making throughout the years should have been good, but I only remember her always saying during the time, "are you done yet?" I tried, or thought I did, to be a good husband. I was never the father to her son that he needed me to be. Obviously, I was never the husband to her she needed me to be also. It turned out this was an uphill battle. My only-child selfishness showed through frequently. Shortly after I got a new job, we talked and decided another divorce was going to happen. She wanted out of the marriage to be free to go after her own goals. I was holding her back.

Here I was again in a lonely situation. I was dealing with lost love, trying to quit smoking, and dealing with the money issues caused from mismanagement, and my failure to be in charge. It is wrong of me to place any blame on her for anything alone. She shared with me once that she had a concern if my daughter ever came into our lives. This was something she didn't want, and she let me know it, but she had never met her. One time when I was active in the Mason's, I was next in line to be the Master of the Lodge and she let me know if I accepted this position, she would come to the public ceremony and make a scene to embarrass me. I never really understood her anger about this, but because I tried to keep peace in the family and save the marriage, I stepped down from this honor. Her father had encouraged her to marry me to give her son a father. Divorce happened and we split ways. Her son was part of my life until the child support stopped when he turned 18. He is very successful today with a PHD in geology. He has chosen not to be a part of my life. The next few years were full of disappointment, sorrow, and loneliness for me until I met my third wife and the Lord, in that order.

My daughter will never know how often I thought of her in those early years. It is hard telling what my daughter's mother said about me when she was young and growing up. Because I hadn't learned forgiveness at this point, all I remembered when I thought of my daughter was the night, I found my wife with another man, and the related anger I carried. I had no money to spare so traveling to Arizona was not possible. After she was newly married at a young age, my daughter reached out to me to tell me she was pregnant and had given birth to a daughter. She had contacted my father to get my contact information, but he said he would contact me and have me get in touch with her. He did, and I did, and today after a rocky start of a relationship, we have a good bond between father and daughter.

This was not a Godly attitude to have but then one has to grow into the walk with God. Some things are easy, and some are not. From a human perspective, we are weak and full of stress. Once you accept the Lord and become a believer, the lessons begin. Life lessons and Godly lessons are entirely different. In life lessons, it's all about self. Pity, guilt, shame, stress, loneliness, and these are only some of the side effects. With God, you learn to deal with life lessons and not be burdened down. With God you learn that Love, Joy, and Peace are fruits of the Spirit and are there to give you hope.

When God is in a relationship, it is meant to be.

I must admit I was sexually active during the years before meeting the true love of my life. I had come to the point where sex was only a temporary fix in searching for happiness. I wanted and needed more. During the spring of 1982, I decided to take a college course at the local community college. I was starting on my way to get the 4-year college education I didn't get at an early age because I had to get a job to support a family. I was taking two courses this term. One was an accounting course, and the other was an elective titled Human Relations in Business and Industry. She sat in the back of the class and was very attractive and always wore skirts to class. She was older than the typical twenty-year-old student and I wanted to meet her. She had the greatest pair of legs. I know, TMI (too much information). Every night of class she would walk past me on her way to get the teacher coffee. I was always in the hallway puffing away on a cigarette but never missed her walk to the coffee machine.

She always sat in the back of the class next to a guy that could have been a boyfriend. I had been rejected m times, so I was reluctant to even talk to her. However, on one night when I was early to class, there she was, alone. I said to myself tonight is the night we are going to talk. I put my book down on my desk and headed back to where she was. When I turned at the end of the row and walked a few more feet towards her, she totally shocked me and said, "the Lord wanted me to tell you that you have the nicest smile". Now what was I to do? I had my line set for how I was going to start this conversation, but it totally escaped me. I know it's going to sound like a square old fashion thing, but the corniest thing came out of my mouth. "Thanks". I then said, wait for it, "blow in my ear and I will follow you anywhere." This simple action brought us together and the relationship adventure started. She was an old fashion girl who loved God and did not believe premarital sex was His plan for a believer of Christ. In her mind, intercourse was never considered until marriage.

On our first date, this subject came up. First, she told me about a recent situation where a guy she had been dating, broke a date with her to do something with his old girlfriend. She was clearly upset because they were going to go to her high school reunion together. She had even been taking dancing lesson with him for this event. Because we were together now at dinner, she asked me would I like to go with her to the reunion. This was the first date, so I wanted to be sure she liked me as much as I liked her and not just a first choice for a date after her rejection from the other guy. I don't remember how I said it, but I suggested we wait until the evening was over to see if she still wanted me to go with her. In her mind, her first thought was, and I quote, "if you are going out with me for sex, forget it. I am not that kind of girl!" Wow. It wasn't a thought I had, but it was refreshing to hear this. We had a long discussion over dinner sharing where we both were in life and what our goals were at that time. When the evening was over and I took her home, she quickly said to me, "well, are you going to the reunion with me or not?" I immediately told her I would be honored to be her date at this event. Later, after we were married, she asked why I said what I did that night. I told her I wanted her to have an out and change her mind if she didn't like me. I needed to be loved and didn't want her to be in a relationship, even for a date, where she would rather be with someone else other than me. Having had two broken marriages, rejection was something I wanted to avoid if possible.

This has probably been too much background of

my life, but I feel it is necessary to point out that every caregiver has a life before assuming this responsibility. Yes, at times life is hard, and can be funny at the same time. If you accept the fact God knows the plans he has for you, and you grow from the experiences, you become a better person. We never learn the lessons which are without problems or cares. We learn from our mistakes. And yes, the events I went through, and I am sure any reader of this book will relate to some of this back story, made me the person I am today. I'm still learning life's lessons and trying hard to be the best caregiver I can be, with God's help.

From this moment on, my life changed. I wanted what this woman had, and I wanted her to love me if that was possible. In July of 1982 she led me to the Lord. Life really changed after this point. I proposed to her a few weeks later, and she said yes. We married in September of that year and life has been wonderful. See my other published book titled "A Woman's Walk with God" for more on our marriage of 39 years and counting. To easily find it, search for me as the author on Amazon.com. Our story is a true love story and God has walked with us through it all. For many years my wife journaled her life and documented the many times God answered prayer. If you want to be blessed, please read the other book also.

Many years later my father apologized to me for not being the father he should have been. I told him I missed spending time with him growing up, but I learned how much love he had for my mother and his devotion to her was a large lesson for me. I was selfish as an only child and his sacrifice taught me what true love is. I thanked him for being a man I could look up to and would try to be as loving as he was.

CHAPTER THREE: WHAT IS A CAREGIVER?

As the name implies, it is giving care to another person. One of the basic lessons we learn at an early age is to be as nice to others as you would have them be nice to you. The bible also tells us to "do unto others as you want them to do unto you". A cynical person goes through life trusting no one and turns this basic thought around to read "do unto others before they do it unto you". Most of us do not expect to be called upon to give care to another. As we look at relationships, especially marriage, the vows two people take together is 'to have and to hold from this day forward, for better or for worse, for richer, for poorer, in sickness and in health, to love and cherish, till death us do part.' If you are serious about this vow, you both agree to be a care giver should the need arise. While the marriage vows are spoken later in life as an adult, all relationships should have the same purpose or meaning if they are to last. Being there for a friend in their time of need shows your Christian love for them and willingness to be there for others.

I had no clue at an early stage in my life that I would again in later years be called on to be a caregiver. This time it would be for my best friend, my lover, and my wife. As a born-again believer today, I know the

Father knew the plans He had for me even before I was born. Today I depend on the promises in the bible to get me through every day.

When I married my wife, I also became part of a larger southern family I learned to love. As an only child I was intimidated by the love and family ties siblings enjoyed. Let me say no family is perfect and the southern family I married into was no different. Yes, they squabbled on occasion and yes, the drinkers and non-drinkers had their own cliques. But they knew what family was and what that meant. I was excepted and loved also even though I was a northerner. Those closest in age to me are the brothers and sisters I never had. My wife was one of seven. By the time we married, one sister and one brother had already passed away. The oldest sister was 10 years older and the middle sister was 5 years older than my wife. For many years we would travel to Tennessee for the family reunion which always took place on the weekend after Labor Day. Everyone brought food if they could, and for three hours the family shared a great time together at the Kentucky Lake State Park outside of Paris Tennessee. This was a great place and centrally located for most to come to.

Health issues for this family, as with many families were always there. My wife's oldest sister has dementia but remains pretty healthy in spite of it. Her hearing is mostly gone but she is alert. Her oldest brother was diagnosed with Alzheimer's and lived about 3 years after the diagnosis. In his case he eventually got physically angry and was a handful for his wife and family to care for. One night he forgot how to breathe and passed away in his sleep. He was a Baptist preacher and read his bible right up to the very end. Some of the stories he told to those willing to listen, claimed he knew were true were because he was there. For example, in the bible, Lot's wife was turned into a pillar of salt when she turned to witness the fall of her hometown. The Lord had said to do so, (turn to see the town burn) would result in this happening. She turned anyway and the result was as warned. Her brother said he witnessed this happening because he was there. Another story involved a news report about O.J. Simpson being accused of killing his ex-wife. Her brother again claimed he was at the spot of the killing. He said he remembers getting out of the service and he and his buddies were at this gate in question where the crime occurred. He said he had tried to open the gate and it was his blood on the latch. The reason this happened he said, was because the gate was stuck and wouldn't open, and he accidentally cut his hand trying to open it. He never claimed any other detail about this fateful event or that he saw it happen. The real fact is, it was many years before this event took place when he was released from the army, compared to the time of the OJ trial. This was not possible, but in his mind, he was there.

There are many publications about dementia one can read to understand what might be going on in the mind of a person having this disease. Dementia is the big umbrella under which specific symptoms are included. Three of the different types are addressed and included in a brochure with a subtitle _Recognizing when it is not Parkinson's or Alzheimer's disease_ submitted by the Lewy Body Dementia (LBD) Association in 2014. I feel it is important to include a summary as printed of these findings here to help others in understanding what severe dementia is about. The early differentiating twelve symptoms addressed are as follows:

1. Decline in thinking abilities that interferes with everyday life.
    a. LBD: Always

    b. Alzheimer's: Always

    c. Parkinson's: Possible years after diagnosis

2. Significant memory loss.

    a. LBD: Possible

    b. Alzheimer's: Always

    c. Parkinson's: Possible years after diagnosis

3. Planning or problem-solving abilities.

    a. LBD: Likely

    b. Alzheimer's: Possible

    c. Parkinson's: Possible

4. Difficulty with sense of direction or spatial relationships between objects.

    a. LBD: Likely

    b. Alzheimer's: Possible

    c. Parkinson's: Possible

5. Language Problems.

    a. LBD: Possible

    b. Alzheimer's: Possible

    c. Parkinson's: Possible

6. Fluctuating cognitive abilities, attention or alertness.

    a. LBD: Likely

    b. Alzheimer's: Possible

    c. Parkinson's: Possible

7. Changes in Mood.

    a. LBD: Possible

    b. Alzheimer's: Possible

    c. Parkinson's: Possible

8. Hallucinations:

    a. LBD: Possible

    b. Alzheimer's: Unlikely

    c. Parkinson's: Possible

9. Severe sensitivity to medications used to treat hallucinations.

    a. LBD: Likely

    b. Alzheimer's: Unlikely

    c. Parkinson's: Possible

10. Changes in walking or movement, such as slower, smaller steps, problems using hands, tremors.

    a. LBD: Possible

    b. Alzheimer's: Unlikely

    c. Parkinson's: Always

11. Balance problems and/or falls.

    a. LBD: Possible

    b. Alzheimer's: Unlikely

    c. Parkinson's: Possible

12. Rapid eye movement (REM) sleep behavior disorder.

    a. LBD: Possible

    b. Alzheimer's: Unlikely

    c. Parkinson's: Possible

More information about the Lewy Body Dementia Association can be found at their web site lbda.org. More information on Parkinson's is also available here.

Memories are a funny thing. Dementia and Alzheimer's directly impacts a person's memory recall. My wife can remember things that happened when she was five years old but forgets ten minutes later after she had eaten lunch, that she ate, what she ate, or that someone was here visiting and left. She would often say how did I miss them being here or I don't remember going to church and hearing the Pastor preach. As a caregiver it is important to always provide positive feedback especially when something confusing has happened. Do not ever call them names or say they are stupid. If you get frustrated over this happening, seek outside help for them. You are not doing them any good if this is your reaction to their confusion. Sometimes, if I remember, I will take a picture of someone who has been here so when this happens, and it happens a lot, I can show her the picture and it satisfies the missing memory, or at least defuses the state of confusion. My goal is to provide a positive happy environment to minimize frustration. This is not always possible but for the most part, it works for me.

Every person requiring care has needs very different from anyone else. There are many reasons why care is needed. In my case, I am only addressing the needs associated with dementia and specifically Alzheimer's. Regardless of why the need for care exists, the role of a caregiver is basically the same. Learn to help and do for another the things they used to do for themselves but can't do it anymore. The role of a caregiver is not for everyone. Have your eyes open when you assume this role and be prepared to do it if your physical and mental health remains good. Also, be prepared to ask for help because at some point, you will get burned out. Seek advise from family and friends and outside counselling if necessary. Seeking and walking with the Lord has worked the best for me.

CHAPTER FOUR: WHAT ALZHEIMER'S IS NOT

Every person who has Alzheimer's has unique reactions to events around them. One of the hardest situations to deal with is when a thought comes and there is a desire to share or say something but the process to articulate the need is not there. Frustration sets in when they can't formulate the details of the thought in order to share it. You can sense their frustration, but no matter what, know there is no way to help them to regain the initial thought because you are not in their head. You can never know where they think they are or what it is they want to do. The best thing is to change the subject and hope the frustration leaves. My wife had an Aunt who also had Alzheimer's and she eventually was placed in a home because she could not take care of herself. She would often forget names of close family but knew she loved them. The question is, did she recognize them or was she just grateful for any visitor. After being in the nursing home, she often just sat around staring out into space. Keeping the person being cared for at home is the best when it is possible because it is a familiar happy place.

As the disease continues to consume, the progression is slow on a daily basis. I am a believer happiness is the best medicine. When the disease is first diagnosed there aren't many symptoms other than memory loss. As we age we all have moments where we forgot some one's name or where we left our car keys. How about when we go into a room of the house and wonder why we are there. Could this be an early sign of dementia? Maybe. Early in 2013 the doctors found by God's divine intervention, an aneurism on the aorta blood vessel in her brain, right between her eyes, three inches into her head. The doctors said we could do nothing but if it burst, it could kill her. After further review and tests, the doctors determined it had a daughter aneurism also which meant the possibility it could burst is even further escalated. After much prayer we decided to have the surgery. The doctors went into the head and clipped the aneurism so it couldn't burst. Eight days in ICU recovery was very hard but bearable. Prior to this surgery we both have the typical 'old timers' memory' issues. Forgetting names was the norm. After the surgery things started getting worse. Nothing of any real concern at the start. After coming home from the hospital, she was convinced the condo we lived in in Frankenmuth was not the same one we lived in before her surgery. I assured her this was not the case, but I don't think she ever accepted what I told her. Later in 2013, we moved to be closer to the immediate family.

As time passed little things came to light. I started reading up on dementia and Alzheimer's and the symptoms. I read that Alzheimer's can't really be diagnosed until after death. However, certain events started happening causing concern. The biggest situation occurred on a trip to Florida when we were separated going through security. Here we were in a large airport unfamiliar to both of us. I was delayed getting released from security and when I did, she wasn't at the end of the security area waiting for me. I panicked because I had no idea where she was. She could have been in a bathroom or at another place in the airport where I wasn't. There was plenty of time before the flight was scheduled to leave, but my stress levels went through the roof because I couldn't find her. Perhaps I was being over-protective, but it scared me to pieces. Yes, I prayed but didn't give it to God. I worried even more. After hours it seemed, probably no more than 20-30 minutes, I found her sitting in a waiting area looking and waiting for me. I was so relieved to have found her. She wasn't worried or showing any signs of stress. I took it all upon myself.

Even recalling this memory for this story, my anxiety rises just thinking about this situation. I made up my mind then this can't happen again. It was obvious there were other issues, but I didn't want to put a name on it. Perhaps I didn't want to face reality. Our family doctor recommended I have her tested by a medical group specializing in dementia cases. I was reluctant to agree to the test. When we got back from Florida, we resumed doing normal things. She had a vehicle and would often go to the thrift stores by herself. She told me she got turned around one day and rode for an hour in the country trying to get home. She made it but then I knew I had to do something. Rather than having her forget where we lived or how to get to a friend's house, I asked the doctor to set up a referral to have the appropriate tests done.

The test was scheduled a few weeks later and when called into the testing process, they let me go in also. The first person she talked to had asked four basic questions. What is your name? What is your birth date? What day is it today? What year is it today? She knew her name but couldn't answer the remaining questions, so I did for her. Obviously, my time with her during this test was limited. I was told they were here to evaluate her, not me. Off to the waiting room I was sent. Two or three hours later she was asked to sit with me in the waiting room. They called her in again after a few minutes rest and for another two hours they tested her on more items. When it was done, I was told they will set up a follow up appointment to review the results.

About 30 days later, they called and we both went. At the doctor's office I asked If I could come in without her to hear the results. They agreed. I was being overprotective, but I didn't want to put a name to this condition. I remember how it was when we discovered the aneurism and wanted to avoid the worry if at all possible. The doctor said she had all the conditions of Alzheimer's. In fact, she was in the late stages of the disease and probably had about three years to live. He said she failed every test except reading. This was a lot to absorb and face alone. I called her son's, and they came over and we discussed the diagnosis together. I believe in full disclosure and no secrets. She was in the room when we had this discussion, but she heard nothing or said nothing about this meeting. Both sons were understanding and said they were thankful I was in her life. Obviously, they had their own lives and family to deal with and really didn't need another burden. Neither of them said this! However, the reality of the situation cannot be minimized. The older son's wife has liver and kidney issues, and the younger son's wife has heart issues. The older son has faithfully visited almost every Wednesday and the younger son comes when he can. I brought my daughter up to date on the situation and she is very supportive, as are the sons. However, she also has health issues and two young children at home to raise. I praise the Lord for giving me the strength to provide the care needed in this situation. Outside of the family, everyone is concerned I will get burned out and not be able to take care of myself either. I am not a martyr, but I have the Lord and He is with me. If I feel the need to get away, a few of our friends have agreed to come in and sit with my wife while I am gone. This doesn't happen very often, so I try to take her with me wherever I need to go.

This brings up another good point. The books on Alzheimer's always say to never leave the person alone because they could walk away and get lost or injured. This is a concern I am aware of, but so far have had no bad experiences yet praise the Lord. I have started ordering groceries online and having the food delivered. On rare occasions, I go to the store and convince her to come in with me to shop. More often than not, she prefers to wait in the car. If it's hot out, I leave the car running so the air conditioning keeps her cool. In the wintertime I leave the car running with the heater on. I know I am breaking all the rules here and every logical thinking person is screaming 'are you nuts to do this?' All she would need to do is to get behind the wheel and take off. Or they might say she could just get out and walk away with no one watching. My wife is at the point she doesn't remember how things work so taking off in the car, while not impossible, is a very slim occurrence to ever happen. She wouldn't know you can't put the car in gear without pressing on the break. Walking away is another issue and I am concerned about this. I pray she would show signs of maybe doing this before it really happens. I do encourage her to go and get the mail at our house. This requires her to walk out of the house about fifty feet to the mailbox and return. This exercise I hope would tell me if she should feel the need to wander off or forget where she was. So far so good and she has always returned pretty quickly. As a caregiver we have to always be alert to potential situations that could create confusion resulting in them making unfamiliar decisions. The person getting the care always needs to know where we are if we leave the room, and we need to know at all times where they are. If they need us, we have to be there for them.

Today she reads but has no comprehension of what she has read. I give her daily bible stories from Guideposts, and she reads them but never shares any revelation from this reading. She is starting to not be able to recognize words and she asks what the word is or how is it pronounced. Patience again is key here. Never act perturbed about responding to a question or a forgotten thought. If this starts to be an issue, you need help to get time for yourself. You cannot be a grudging caregiver and be effective. This is not good for either of you.

The late stage of anything means many different situations for everyone. In our case it meant to prepare for the end. This could mean death or the simple continued decline in the cognitive abilities we often take for granted. The first thing I did was to sell her car and promised I would take her anywhere she wanted to go whenever she wanted. I had heard so many stories about folks getting lost and couldn't find their way home. Prior to this she had shared with me how she had gotten turned around and rode for miles in the country until she found a road she recognized. She thought nothing of this after she was home.

One of the early symptoms was her loss of taste and smell. This is a documented side effect of Alzheimer's. This only created an issue for eating or cooking. I had already assumed all kitchen duties before this came to a head. When we go to a restaurant, she always says to order her something because I know what she likes. It turns out her appetite also changes as time passes. When she sees a picture of food on the TV or in a magazine, she wants it. When I try to oblige, she might eat half of what is before her. Dessert foods like ice cream, and chocolate are always on the menu in her mind. She loves to go on road trips and out to eat. When the COVID-19 hit and the governor shut down all indoor dining, this made things harder. Fast food eaten at home has worked but she enjoys restaurant indoor dining, when the weather is too cold to eat outside.

Finding an activity to give her joy in doing something has been a real interesting adventure. One of the early projects was to complete jig saw puzzles. It was easy to find puzzles with large pieces and reasonable pictures. This worked for many month's until it got to the point where she wanted to put a puzzle piece in a spot that clearly didn't fit, and she pounded it down with her fist. We had probably done 50 or more puzzles before this and she was happy. It's not that she was unhappy in forcing a puzzle piece to fit. She just wanted to put one in a place just to do it. I had even tried puzzles with Christian words thinking she would find the right piece based on making the words fit. It didn't. the next effort was to try bingo. We did this together and it seemed like she was good with it but when she couldn't concentrate on finding a number in six game boards, it was time to give this up too. However, the activity was good for at least six month's or more.

During this time, we were also playing an old card game called Canasta. We have friends from church who liked to play games and cards too, so with some minor help, it seemed she was handling Canasta well. One day I asked her if she had a particular card, like ace of spades, and had no clue what a spade was or an ace. My goal in her care is to avoid frustration in any form when possible. I know I have to let her do as much as she can for herself but when she doesn't know what is needed, I will step in or change directions. Trying to play cards and understanding the rules, wasn't going to happen anymore. She has always enjoyed playing card games, but she forgot she did. We have tried dice games like Farkle and Yahtzee, but she didn't understand why you had to roll the dice. The latest game we have tried is dominos. Playing Mexican train worked for a while, but she couldn't grasp why you couldn't play on all tiles. Of late, we play just open domino's where every tile can be matched. Sometimes she can compare what tiles she has compared to those in front of her and make a play, and at other times she can't mentally grasp the concept of what is required. It is always surprising on every new game of dominos when we say she is to grab 15 tiles. Inevitably, she will grab a lessor amount and has no clue how many more are needed. These are basic skill sets and it is hard to fathom when they are not understood. Being a caregiver is to care and always show love. Having patience is so important and doing so is showing love to the person needing care.

While a caregiver has to sacrifice some of their life to make the patient happy, it must be done with love. Feelings of being a martyr in any caregiving life is not good for anyone. At some point it is time to consider alternatives to how the care is being given and by whom? Ask the family to help when they can and if they are willing. If not willing, understand caregiving is not for everyone, regardless of relationship. Do not hold this against them. Perhaps you need to hire someone to be with the patient to give yourself time away. As long as they are pretty self-sufficient in caring for their basic needs, keeping them at home is the best way to guarantee their happiness. For me this means she must be able to get dressed and doing other personal needs like adding jewelry or combing her hair. She doesn't make decisions, so I get her clothes out and lay them on the bed. Feeding herself is another basic need as is going to the bathroom. I do all the cooking and put food in front of her to eat. When needed she can cut her food into smaller pieces, so this function is still working. However, I have discovered putting smaller pieces on the plate first, she will usually eat everything. A nursing facility should be the last resort, if for no other reason than the cost factor. Also, in my mind, no one can give the level of care I can each and every day.

CHAPTER FIVE: NEEDS ARE DIFFERENT

When a caregiver starts offering a service, the requirements for care is not the same for all those needing care, depending on the type of care required. Regardless, it is hard to see a loved one deal with the difficulties they once could do for themselves. Once diagnosed as having late-stage Alzheimer's is basically saying at some point in time, the brain will forget how to breathe or forget how to swallow which will change and impact continued life on earth. There is no way to prepare for this happening except through prayer. My goal is to keep my wife happy, but not doing things for her she can still do for herself. She will not make decisions on what to wear or what to order in a restaurant. I have assumed this responsibility without regret. I select what she will wear and identify which ear each hearing aid belongs in. Some simple tasks require additional attention.

In the next paragraphs I will describe the many struggles faced. Fortunately, frustration over her current inabilities is not an issue at this point. As time has passed, there has been demonstrated some brief anger issues. Really more like a tantrum, like as small child throws when they don't get their way. She does get bored easily and naps a lot. She enjoys going on short excursions, even if it is only to get lunch and bring it home to eat.

In January, my wife was very angry one morning. To begin with, I hadn't laid out her clothes for the day and she wanted to get dressed. I am usually up before her and have this task done when she awakes. She had decided to wear her housecoat instead of clothes, so she put it on and snapped it up. Then she wanted a scarf. Socks and tennis shoes completed the outfit. When I told her, this outfit was ok around the house, but it wouldn't work to wear out. She got really angry and threw off these clothes, literally. She went back to the bathroom and was ok to get dressed after the tantrum was over. It was like nothing ever happened after ten minutes. I am not used to this anger. It is so not her.

In April, after I had settled her to sleep. I typically take 30 minutes of private time in the bathroom before coming to bed. When I did get to the bed, she woke up and asked me if her mother was in the living room watching TV. I told her she wasn't. She asked, where was she? I told her I didn't know, but I knew she was gone. She said no more and drifted back off to sleep, satisfied her mother was OK and not here. She frequently wakes up momentarily after dreaming about a family member and asks where so and so was. Were they still here or somewhere else in our home? One time she just knew her mother had been in bed with us and wondered where she had gone when she awoke. I decided to never challenge her dream but to respond in a way to give her closure. This might be wrong, but it eliminates the frustration she can have when she can't fix it or deal with it.

Watching NCIS one night, the story line centered around a missing body. When I was trying to tell my wife about the story line and the fact a car blew up, the two details came together in her mind, and she suggested the dead body was in the next commercials mailbox. This made no sense, but she was convinced this could help. This had been an unusually busy day, and she was really tired. She couldn't focus on anything on TV or in what she was reading.

Our good friends understand the issues around this disease and are willing to be patient enough to do whatever it takes to offer diversion to boredom. This has worked for many months until it became obvious, she couldn't focus on what was required when it was her turn to play if we were playing a game. The first sign was her inability to know the difference between the suits of cards or to focus on what or why something was happening in the game. She could handle red versus black and the numbered cards. The face cards became confusing.

We tried bingo at the senior center for a number of months. The smallest set of bingo cards was a sheet of six. For a while this was good mental activity to search for a number when it was called. We stopped playing bingo when she couldn't concentrate long enough to search all six cards for a specific number. It came to a point where she forgot what she was looking for. The positive thing was to keep her out in public and interacting with others but nothing more than casual conversation. When around other people, she basically just sits quietly and listens but doesn't grasp the focus of any discussion nor does she say much. People we are with know this and talk to me and not her. This doesn't seem to be a problem because it doesn't cause any reaction in her.

On occasion we still play dominos with our good church friends. It seems like a simple thing for us, but she can't process the logic or the basic skills to enjoy the game. I feel the game is almost too much for her but as long as she willing to play with help it is good to continue, or is it? Yes, it is an activity but not one she really participates in. Our good church friends have a lot of patience so keeping this going is good. I am a firm believer of keeping social interactions going as long as she is responsive when others talk to her. I know the time will come when she won't respond to any communication. Now, when the dialog is simple and doesn't require any thought, her responses flow.

She loves to go and get out of the house. It can be a short trip to the bank drive through or the fast-food restaurant drive through. Her sons have been very faithful and visit frequently. When I have a commitment to do something, one of them will come and either stay with her or take her on a road trip for a couple of hours. Within a few minutes of returning, she has forgotten she went anywhere and is ready to go again. She recognizes both sons and I make sure to mention their names frequently.

Recently we had a call from the local hospital getting some information regarding a surgical process to remove her gall bladder. This is not a big deal anymore and is considered an outpatient procedure. This hospital does not have in their records the fact we are dealing with Alzheimer's. When I tried to provide the information they needed, they said they needed to have her authorization to talk to me. I put her on the phone, and she said yes, they can talk to me. Then they asked for her to put me back on the line but before she gave me the phone, they asked her what my name is. She couldn't tell them. She knows we are married and that she loves me, and I always tell her I love her too. I always wondered how I would feel if she got to this point. I can see the big picture now and it does not cause me any concern.

There was a situation in the last few years that

occurred when we traveled to Arkansas to visit her oldest sister. We had stopped at a small gas station mini mart to use their bathroom. She went into the bathroom and locked the door. When she was done, she couldn't get the door opened to get out. She didn't remember how the lock worked. The guy in the minimart had called the police because he needed help to get her out and he didn't realize I was in the parking lot waiting for her to return. In the meantime, I realized she was gone for a long time, so I went into the store to discover what was wrong. When I went in, I quickly figured out there was a problem. The store employee was trying to break the door handle to get it opened to no avail. As I was talking to her through the door, the police showed up. I finally got her to twist the knob of the door which released the lock. However, the police didn't understand the situation and they were ready to lock me up as an abusive husband because she could have used the bathroom to get away from me. It took ten minutes for them to feel good about letting her back into my care, and it turned out ok. However, it was scary for a while and I understood where the police were coming from and their need to clarify the truth in this situation. I made up my mind to always go in with her in the future and guard the door rather than take a chance on her locking it and not being able to open it.

One simple fact I learned from this was to not leave her alone unless she was in a familiar setting. As time passes, I learn from my mistakes because situations like this have happened over and over, but always different each time. This familiar setting could be the grocery store parking lot or the bank. If she recognizes where she is, she is all right for a short time. Leaving her alone for short periods of time is one situation I am watching very closely and carefully assessing those times when I do leave her alone. One time we volunteered to help our church with highway trash pickup. I parked the car on the highway and we both took off together to pick up trash. There were six of us doing this on both sides of the road. My wife got tired after about a half mile into the two mile stretch and she asked to go back to the car. I told her this was OK, but I wanted to go just a little bit farther and would join her soon. I watched to be sure she got back to the car ok and get inside. I went a little further and my spirit was quickened, and I knew I had to return to her soon. I immediately turned around and went back to the car, but it took some time to walk the distance back. Her words to me when I got back to her have been burned in my mind. She said, "I have never felt so alone". I said to myself then, never again. This kind of stress could cause permanent emotional damage and possible health related issues. High stress can cause strokes in senior adults.

Even though I said this, I do occasionally leave her in the car if I need a few things from the grocery store, but I don't leave her if I feel there is a problem or any reluctance in her mind if I do this. So far, she has not felt the need to wander off, nor has there been a problem in sitting and waiting for me. I know this is a possible action of a person with Alzheimer's, so I am being careful to be sure I never leave her alone more than a few minutes. If she ever left the car in this situation at the grocery store or any place and didn't remember where she was, I know she couldn't find her way back home because she never remembers even which car is ours when we leave it and return to it, let alone where we live. This could be church, grocery store, or any place where there are more cars in a lot together. I tell her to go to the white one because she is never sure which white one unless I am next to her. I did get her a medical bracelet that has her name and address embossed along with the phone numbers of the family.

Yesterday, we got back from the hospital where she had outpatient surgery to remove her gall bladder. We were sitting on the loveseat watching TV and I asked how she felt. Fine she said, why? I said to her, "you just had surgery to remove your gall bladder. Does anything hurt?" "Nothing hurts" she said. "Did I really have that done today?" I told her you did, and we were at the hospital for over 6 hours. The nursing staff was concerned because your breathing looked like there was an issue from being under an anesthetic. They put you on oxygen and wouldn't let you go home until your blood oxygen level got above 90. Finally, they let me see you and I assured them your breathing was normal even though it looked like you were struggling to breathe. My wife had a blank look after I told her all of this because she didn't understand what I was talking about. She quickly tuned me out and continued watching TV.

A few moments later I was trying to connect the TV to CBS All Access. As I was working through the steps, she asked if she could help me. The TV screen had a code needing to be added to my smart phone to make the connection work. She pointed to her magazine and said I could add the article she was pointing at to the TV message to make it work. She was sincere in her making this comment and felt it would work. It would have accomplished nothing to make a big deal out of her comment or to say it wouldn't work. I just simply said I almost had it done and was careful not to just ignore her. I thanked her for the input and suggestion. Having her be frustrated over anything is not the way to be helpful to her. After all, she only wanted to help me even though her concept of how this could happen was not understood.

She often has started to want to formulate a thought for something but can't pull the details together to be able to share it. It might be something she wants to do or something needing to be fixed in her mind. She does read a lot and a picture in a magazine might trigger this thought but then the frustration hits because she can't piece together what is needed next. She can't find the words to describe what she wants, and she just sits in a quandary wondering what to do. When this happens, I try to see what she was doing before this thought came to her and usually, I can't determine what it was, and consequently the feeling is lost without resolution. So far, the associated frustration with this action is gone within minutes, like her memory of anything going on around her. She frequently forgets soon after someone has left the house or room that they were even here at all. This could even be her son's.

The evening routine is about the same every night. At 9:00 pm I turn TV off and we head for the bedroom. After being awake for a long time, the bedtime process to get ready doesn't exist without me. If I did not help her with this process she would just go to bed with clothes, shoes, and jewelry on. She wouldn't take her evening pills or even take out her dentures. It's not that she doesn't understand what we do to get ready for bed, it's more like why bother. It's like making the bed every day. Why make the bed every morning when in 12 hours or so we will be right back getting into bed to sleep again. I tell her we do it because God said to do it. The bible reports Jesus said, "get up, make your bed, and go out and serve the Lord". So, we do it too. Even though this is what we do daily, it is not a remembered process in her mind. It makes no sense to even discuss these processes, but it is necessary to keep them up. Would it make a difference to her, no. However, as caregiver, it keeps me grounded. If I didn't do them, there is no one else here to do it. While once we were a team of two with God in the background, now we are a team of three. Me, her, and God and He gives me the strength to carry on during this difficult time.

So far sleeping is not a problem. Many things I read warn of people staying up all night and getting into all kinds of things and hurting themselves. The evening process begins the same way. When we get to the bedroom, the first thing I do is to shut the door to the bedroom and lock it. Not because I am afraid someone might enter but because the lock makes a distinct noise when the door is opened. Just in case I also have Christmas bells hanging from the doorknob to wake me up should the door open. I quickly get her water glass and pills out, grab the denture cup, and start removing her jewelry. My goal is to keep her continually doing something until she is ready for sleep. I place her clothes on the dresser for the next day if she is wearing the same thing. I make sure her hearing aids and earrings are in a small plate on her dressing table. She likes to keep her socks on and her bra on for warmth. She has a night shirt she likes to also put on most of the time. I make a quick check of what has been removed and when she is ready to lay down, I cover her up, raise the head of the bed about two inches and turn on the heating blanket. After a quick kiss goodnight, I head for the bathroom for a short time of peaceful solitude. So far, she sleeps eight to twelve hours every night.

Routine is a way I have found to keep her happy and not frustrated. You might say how could any 'routine' work if her short term memory is only minutes long? It is not what she remembers or not, it is what works to keep her at peace. For example, playing Christian music after breakfast. She really likes Christian songs sung by Elvis. She can remember some of the words for the older hymnal songs. We sit at the table and she reads, and I do my thing on the computer, and we sing together with Elvis. This process takes us to lunch time. During the afternoon after lunch, she naps for about an hour in her easy chair. TV is typically not on until two or three and I have discovered cartoons give her joy to watch. I prefer dramas typically shown at night. Cop shows, action movies, or science fiction. During the holidays we watch a lot of Christmas movies.

I have discovered she can watch any drama but does not understand what is going on. We watched a PBS program yesterday called Death in Paradise. When it was over, I asked her what she thought, and she said didn't remember what she watched. Some things I have read about Alzheimer's suggest what is watched on TV often plants a seed of any type of action in their minds which could have negative results to her or those around her. Anger issues and violent tendencies could by encouraged by what was watched on TV. This could be an issue considering I enjoy watching action programs and she likes sitting next to me holding hands. While I do not discount the warnings, I feel every one's reaction to the disease is unique. For us, at this point I don't see this is a concern. She watches but doesn't see. She has no reaction to whatever we had just watched. I will not be stupid and ignore the possibilities there could be an issue in the future depending on what was watched. I am prepared to react to whatever is needed in any given situation. Her comprehension of what she sees, or reads is gone.

During the night, there have been occasion's when she will wake me up and ask if her mother was here or had already left. I never had the privilege of meeting her mother and rather than cause her frustration over a dream, I respond and assure her she is not here. There are many times when she feels someone is in the house with us and she asked if 'he' has left? I ask who she thinks is here. She doesn't know but remembers there have been men here at different times living in our lower level. Our grandson lived with us for a year and our nephew lived with us three weeks. Our friends from Florida spent a few weeks with us and Tennessee relatives also spent a week once. It is fully finished and a comfortable space to live in away from home. Many of our family and friends have spent time in the lower level living area. When she thinks someone might be here, I assure her we are the only ones here. Depending on how she explains her concern, I might respond and say he or she has left and gone home, or I might just say it's just you and me now. I always want to be certain she feels safe and not frustrated. I try to never just dismiss her concern, even though there is nothing to support it, except a memory that once was there.

My wife is a very loving person and has always liked helping others. We frequently tell each other 'I love You' and we hold hands a lot. Touching is her love language. If she didn't have this her life would change dramatically. She is always amorous and loving and knows I love her too. I tell her we have been married for 39 years and she smiles and says she loves me. She enjoys touching my hand and counting my fingers. Weird in a way but it is a loving thing for her. I will do whatever it takes to keep her happy and not frustrated. I know, based on what I have read, more change is coming. To what degree, only God knows. I bought a golf cart this winter in anticipation of taking rides in the woods when the weather permits. We have tried walking, but her endurance isn't there anymore. We can make a couple of hundred yards and then she wants to go back home. I know exercise is important to keep us healthy but for her it is limited, especially at the age of 82. On rare occasions I have convinced her to come into the grocery store with me, and she will, but gets tired quickly and looks for a place to sit down. With the COVID-19 pandemic, most of the sitting areas around the stores have been removed to prevent the spreading of virus germs. There is no way to expect the store to wipe down every sitting area after someone spends time resting. I am hoping the golf cart will give us new opportunities to go to the nearby lake and perhaps have picnics on occasion. We will see once the weather breaks. Only time will tell.

The bottom-line goal is to keep her at home where she feels safe and with someone who really cares for her. I have always said my goal is to keep her happy. Watching television is an interesting time. She listens but often does not understand what is going on. If we watch a movie that has subtitles, she can never read them fast enough before they are gone, and another string of words appear. Avoiding subtitles is a must in picking movies. Whether good or bad, within 10 minutes she has forgotten what she saw on a program. I might laugh at a commercial or some line spoken in a program and when I ask if she thought it was funny too, she has no idea what I am talking about. Her cognitive abilities are fading fast. What I mean by this is she can read but not understand what purpose the string of words mean, or why they are there. When watching a TV drama, trying to understand the theme of the program or why the actors are doing what they are doing, is gone. We spend a lot of time watching golf. As the players putt and the ball heads for the hole, she will comment if it goes in or just misses. Watching the live action in golf is relaxing for both of us.

CHAPTER SIX: FINDING PEACE

We can sit at the dining room table for hours reading a magazine or a Guideposts publication. Every day, she asks me at least once what a word is she doesn't understand. Her ability to recognize words is getting more and more difficult. There are times when a word just doesn't make sense in an article or story. Her goal is to read every word on the page. On some ads, there are a lot of fine print disclaimers about something, or that something purchased has shipping charges needing to be added. It makes no difference to her. If the words are there, she is determined to read them all. She looks at the pictures in magazines and the caption associated to it. If it is often not clear enough to explain why the picture is there. In one article recently in People magazine, she saw a picture of an actress striking a seductive pose, but not showing any offensive body parts, and the caption did not tell the reader why she had allowed this picture to be taken. In this case, the actress was showing off her 50-year-old body and it was looking as good as some 25-year old's. She could not grasp what this meant. Trying to explain why this was in the magazine and the purpose of why it was there, was like talking to the wall. Frequently, when she reads Guideposts, there is a page advertising a product. She will read this page down to the smallest of print but not recognize it for what it is. She might say to me she 'can't deal with this so please fix it'. I am not sure what her mind wanted me to do. Did she want me to order this item or fix something so she could understand better what the ad was saying. Often times, I will say, "ok, I will check it out". Then I turn the page and give her back whatever she was reading. Her concern was gone, and life moves forward. Trying to rationalize any subject is lost. A few minutes after the fact, the mind is already dealing with the next thing.

Trying to keep organization around us gives some stability to the thinking process. For example, starting every day with breakfast. You might think this is no big deal, but on those occasions when we don't do breakfast first thing, the day is full of moments of confusion and wild daydreams. Tiredness occurs more frequently when the routine is mixed up. I try to provide a banana and a bowl of cereal every morning. The type of cereal is not a big deal. It could be the favorite, Cinnamon Squares, or maybe oats. On top of all this, I am trying to get our weight under control. To make this happen slowly, I find if a lite lunch is provided, a protein drink will frequently satisfy any hunger cravings. While routine is still a goal, meals typically happen at 8am, noon, and 5 pm. We don't typically snack, so this is good. I save a piece of chocolate for a 7pm treat which has worked well so far. Giving up everything we like to eat is not the way to lose weight and keep it off, at least not for us. Frequently, the remembrance of eating is gone a few minutes after eating. This could be bad if a feeling of hunger persists. This is typically not an issue, but it seems when over half of the TV commercials are advertising food by showing the item ready to be eaten, plants a seed of desire in the mind which, in this case, passes quickly.

Recognizing a feeling of hunger might exist, I always ask, "can I get you anything?," The response is typically no, but it looked good enough to eat. Temptation is how many of these companies sell their products. I have discovered ice cream is a real draw. It is obvious one can eat ice cream at any time of the day. It doesn't have to be a lot, just some ice cream with chocolate. I have discovered Klondike Bars satisfy as much as a Dairy Queen cone dipped in chocolate. As humans we all have our comfort foods we like to eat. Psychologically it leaves us with a feeling of satisfaction or happiness. Ice cream does just like chocolate does with many people. As with many things, minutes after consuming the treat, it was forgotten that any ice cream was eaten.

As you may gather, eating is a major issue. With Alzheimer's, one of the well documented symptoms associated with this disease is loss of smell and taste. Putting food on a plate that looks as good as the television commercials, creates a happy feeling and a readiness to eat. A plain burger patty or plain hot dog presented in a healthy way without buns can result in not eating all of the meal, or not eating it all. I wonder if the mind sees the food and says this food doesn't look good, so why eat? I am trying to limit the consumption of bread. The eating situation could be a problem if wandering in the kitchen to look for something to eat was there, but it's not. Prior to the start of seeing symptoms related to the disease, I rarely cooked any meals. Today, the kitchen is my domain and there are no concerns for not cooking anymore. I am occasionally asked if I need help, but I always state I have it under control. I have given her simple tasks to help with a meal but even the ability to understand what is needed to be accomplished in the process is lost. How can we forget how to peel a potato or with what type of tool? I do not understand how this can be after doing all the cooking for 75 years.

It is difficult for anyone around a person with Alzheimer's to truly understand how their mind works. Our bodies are unique and our minds capable of so much when we apply ourselves. I remember as a high school student I was often told I had so much ability to do well in school, but I didn't apply myself. I didn't like High School and my grades showed it. I think it was because I had to be there. There was no choice in this except to quit school, which I did. Later in life, I finished High School and started taking college courses with the hopes of getting a four-year degree. In college, I got straight A's. The difference in college, I was older of course, but I wanted to be there, and I enjoyed learning.

With Alzheimer's, many memories are lost in the memory banks of the brain, as is the memory of cooking. It is like the delete button was pushed in the mind to erase these memories. Today, there is no remembrance of how to even turn on the stove or operate the microwave, let alone remember an old family recipe. As caregivers, we need to accept where they are and help them deal with the things they can do. Eventually, the ability to do the basic things go away. As time passes, I can see more and more simple abilities start to slip away.

Today, we sat at the dining room table where many hours are spent reading while I am working on the computer. Before sitting this morning, the chair had to be in the perfect place. The chair was examined for a few minutes, pushing it in and then pulling it out to get it in the perfect position. When I saw frustration building up, I pulled the chair back a little and suggested sitting and then pulling the chair up to a comfortable position. This happened and I was given thanks for being so helpful. Such a simple task but difficult when you don't feel comfortable doing it.

I have accepted the kitchen responsibilities without any problem. I struggle most with trying to find things to eat. If something on the plate at a meal doesn't look appealing, it is like a child who picks around the food until deciding they are done because they are full. When that happens, I know I could put a dessert item on the plate, and it would be devoured. Too funny.

Being a caregiver is making sure the care you are giving meets the demands of the person being cared for. It's not always what you think is best for them, but what brings them happiness and peace in the long run. A care givers role is to provide the comfortable requirements wanted and needed, without physically placing unreasonable burdens on the person being cared for. However, it needs to be said that once this attitude of the caregiver is lost or becomes a burden to the care giver, it's time to get help. This is not a sign of weakness or giving up. These days, a condition of PTSD (post-traumatic stress disorder) exists with many individuals who have endured any type of physical trauma to themselves or have seen others suffering. A care giver can also have PTSD. It's all about the stress it takes to care for another and often giving up things for yourself. You need to stay healthy physically and mentally to be effective in the care you provide.

I have discovered music calms and creates a peaceful spirit. I will frequently turn on Christian songs by Elvis Presley and we sing together when we know the words. This is a happy time. All music seems to be calming during a time when the need to move around isn't desired. Frequently, going somewhere, if for no other reason than a ride in the country, is also calming. In our case, Christian music works best while at home, but I wonder if it is only the music itself, not the words in the song. Listening, but not hearing is often the norm. At times, when the words to a song is known, we sing along joyfully. This seems to be a therapeutic exercise.

The same is true with television. Understanding when a commercial is on to sell something and it uses a unique setting to set the mood to entice a future purchase, the purpose of the commercial is often misunderstood, and the reality compared to today cannot be determined. This is especially true if the ad is animated. I can ask her if she wants what is being advertised, if it is food, and she has no clue what was being advertised. A young child, and even adults, can often be convinced of something once they see an example of something or a response to an event. A subliminal message is often missed by logical reasoning because we don't physically see it. It is like planting a seed in the garden. Once planted, it grows if watered. This is often the purpose of some commercials. Does the mind that listens and sees, hear and retain good or bad thoughts? It is like the issue of homosexuality. More and more the primetime TV programs include homosexuals kissing or holding hands. Society today and mainstream media is trying to convince us this is normal and should be accepted. As Christians, we know what the Bible has to say about homosexuality and we are taught to love the sinner, not the sin. As humans, we are impressionable animals. We know what we see impacts us and causes us to react to certain events when they happen. But does it in the mind of a person with Alzheimer's? They read but don't comprehend what has been read. If an old-time western movie is watched and the soldiers are fighting Indians and people are being killed. Does this plant a seed in the mind that killing is right? To some it might because it happened and was part of the history of our nation. To some with Alzheimer's, it is not a recorded happening. It is only movement on the TV. They watch but don't see or at least their minds can no longer process what it is they are watching.

Memory retention of something read or seen on television does not appear to be the case today. If I turn on an animated program, it almost feels like watching a real live person, or so it seems based on a response to a question I might pose. As caregiver, I feel it is important to encourage them to do as much as possible for themselves without help. I think this encouragement gives them a purpose in living. There are many things that can't be done anymore, so I will do them to help. However, it is necessary to wait until a decision is made in their mind something can't be done before I step in. The ability to recognize some big words when reading frequently results in asking me what the word is. I tried to help by sounding out the word like we have done in training a young person how to read. My effort, even though it was meant for good, is not always received that way.

On one occasion, my help turned out to be a disaster and she quickly said forget it and moved on to another part of what was being read. I knew this was counterproductive so now when asked what a word is, I repeat it but also offer a definition of the word. For example, reading about the COVID-19 vaccines being distributed, the word 'inoculation' was used in the paragraph and it was not recognized. I pronounced the word and told her it was used to describe getting a shot in the arm to prevent us from getting the COVID-19 disease as bad as it could be if not inoculated. The answer was accepted, and she went back to what was being read. Do I think any part of the explanation I provided was retained or learned? Probably not, but the frustration that could have been felt was not realized.

Recently while looking out the window, it was

felt it was critical for us to go now and get our car. I surmised the thought was there that the car was somewhere for repairs and it was ready to be picked up. I explained the car was in the garage and it was fine so there was no need to go and do this. This satisfied the concern for about fifteen minutes but then again decided we just had to go now and do it. Frustration was setting in, and because I try my best to avoid this if possible, I said OK, let's go for a ride. We left and I intentionally stopped where she thought the car was and again tried to explain the car we were in was our only car today. This seemed to take care of the issue.

There are many normal things in daily life no longer can be done. It's hard to know what the best approach is in dealing with this. Should we always encourage the person needing care to try and do whatever the need might be, themselves. Or is this a desire in futility hoping they will again learn how to do something they appear not able to do. Recently while playing dominos with friends, they said to me to let her play the tiles herself rather than help her. Our friend informs me she has experience working with Alzheimer's patients and this is the way to best help them. So, I sit back reluctantly and don't assist in helping right away to identify what tile to play next. When it was announced there is no where to play a tile, it was hoped the play would pass to the next person. In fact, there were many places to play one of the tiles. I try to explain how it works and all that is needed is to do is to match the end of one of the tiles to one already on the table. The ability to see where a match might be is difficult. I decided to point out where there are two or three plays that could be made and then let them decide where to play a tile. When a play is made, the wife acknowledges out loud, "good job". I'm not sure this is positive approach. It is only a game, but so is life. We know life's lessons brought before us by God and when we fail to learn what we need to deal with a situation, He will give them to us again until we do learn. This is especially true in dealing with people.

Examine your own relationships in the past and you can see how this statement is true. You may not acknowledge God and the fact he does have a role in your lives but someday, in hindsight, you might. This is another topic for another book. When you praise someone for doing a good thing or in this case finding a place to play a tile, you hope this reinforcement will encourage them to do more by themselves. The difference is the lack of finding a match to place a tile is not because of laziness or being tired. The ability to see the table where other tiles are played and rationalize where a match might be just isn't there anymore. Our friends mean well, but in this case, I am not sure it is helping.

One thing I have decided I need to deal with is the possibility I might not be around long enough to continue the care I want to be certain my wife gets. She is 82 years old and I am 76. We are both pretty healthy, but we do have underlying health conditions. What happens if I should pass before she does? Our days are numbered by God and anyone of us might not see another ten minutes or another day. With this thought in mind, I have compiled a list of those things I feel she can no longer do for herself. Thinking perhaps if one of her son's or my daughter steps forward to continue her care, this list might help them meet her needs. Even if a nursing home facility was the solution, they could use this list also. I feel no one could give the care I want provided, but then I love her, and we have been together for 39 years, for better or worse. However, I do not feel this is the worse. For me, worse has yet to happen. Life however has happened.

The daily things done without help seem few. Dressing in the morning works if clothes are laid out. Eating without help is still good but she can't cook. Reading People Magazine and Guideposts literature still happens, but the same pages are read over and over like it is the first time seen. Reading without comprehension is reality. Music is enjoyed and singing Christian songs, especially those sung by Elvis Presley is fun. Remembering the words to many of the old church hymns is still there. Doing the normal bathroom things without help, unless she has a problem like diarrhea, still is good. Cleaning up a mess is more than she can deal with. If under ware needs to be changed, no knowledge of where to get clean ones exists, so she would go without, rather than ask. Because I have embraced new technology, using the cell phone is a challenge she can't understand. There is no clue how to turn it on or even to make a call. If needed, calling 911 wouldn't happen. Answering a call on the cell phone can't happen because there is no retained ability to know how to do so. Instruction has been given but again nothing retained. If access to a regular home phone existed, every call regardless of who was calling, would be answered. There are so many scams these days using the telephone, and for our general protection, I felt it best to only have one phone. Using the cell phone gives me control of all calls. Out of sight and out of mind makes the missing regular telephone a non-issue. Being left alone can never happen. If she fell, she could never get help by summoning someone. When falling becomes an issue, I will see about getting an emergency button worn around the neck to be pressed if help is needed. When out of my sight for any length of time, I always call out to see if there is a problem. Falling has not been an issue but could be in the future. I always want to be there or have someone there to help her or to get the help if needed.

Writing this last paragraph, I almost feel like I am keeping my wife in bondage. This is not the case. I try to be sure everything is good, and she is happy most of the time. I want to recognize what can and can't be done and try to compensate for these basic needs as required. I try to establish a routine so when things like a shower comes up, it happens with only a little push back. Ah yes, shower time. Now here is a challenge. When you think you don't need a shower on a regular basis is wrong thinking. Keeping the body clean is imperative to good health. Trying to explain this or trying to convince this is a needed process is like talking to the wall sometimes. There are never comments made like "I haven't done anything to get dirty so why do I need to shower?" As with many things, rational discussions on showering, flushing the toilet, and shutting the bathroom door when other people are here, falls on deaf ears. The memory of why something is done or needed to be done is gone.

Today after church was a rough time. On the way home, we took a senior friend to her house and then went on home. On the way I commented that the Pastor was long winded today and had to cut his sermon short because he had already gone over an hour and we had communion yet to do. The comment made was, "I didn't know our Pastor preached today. I don't remember hearing him." This was literally 10 minutes after the sermon ended and 5 minutes after we left the church. I must remember the reality of the situation and when there is a lot of commotion at church and many people we interact with, if for no other reason than saying hello or have a blessed day, is confusing. Dwelling on the subject of who preached or what the message was about is not a win-win situation. Normal conversation, if such a thing exists, it is not there anymore. I guess I am feeling a little frustrated today and I miss the conversation I have enjoyed for 39 years. It is best to just move on and deal with the here and now. Its something new every day.

CHAPTER SEVEN: SUNDOWNER ISSUES

Acknowledging the things, the person needing care can't do anymore by themselves is a critical step in planning for extended care in the future, however long or brief that might be. As this chapter title alludes to is how situations change given the time of the day. By the end of the day, the comment frequently made is "my get up and go, got up and went". The daily activity, or lack thereof, results in being tired but has desire to just rest and be quiet. Following a routine has benefits that can be seen and measured. I

n the evening while we are watching television, there are often complaints asking why banners describing a product or a subtitle so quickly disappear from the screen before they can be read. This is very true with commercials. There are many new drug ads that come with descriptions of benefits and side effects. In trying to read them, because comprehension is fading, confusion results in just trying to understand and figure out what word was displayed. I will frequently pronounce the word hoping it will help, but it results in additional confusion. In the rare occasion when we watch a program having subtitles when the language being spoken is not English, this situation is further exasperated. Watching the action on the screen and trying to read the words is hard and so she often just gives up. What happens then is she just sits quietly watching and maybe listening some, but not hearing or understanding what is going on in the program. Watching the screen movements, I guess is contentment. We watched an old Jerry Lewis movie recently and enjoyed it and laughed at the comedian's antics. Cartoons are also a good choice to watch because there is no deep plot to figure out or a scene to try to understand why it's being showed.

The first thing in the morning she experiences alertness and is responsive to discussions. During our morning prayers, I will often mention needs we are praying for others to receive. Even though memories of who these people are is gone, praying in the Spirit often gives a feeling of reaching out to God. In those cases when she can't identify who we are praying for, I try to have a picture available when this happens so I can show who they are. Sometimes this helps and sometimes it doesn't. The important fact is we pray very sincerely and know we are talking to God. Prayer is a powerful tool and our opportunity to draw near to God. We often recite the comment "God is good all the time; All the time God is good".

We recently experienced a situation where the condo where we live had to have the roof replaced because of hail damage. The insurance covered the cost but the disruption from the noise was unbearable for her. Many have experienced the nervousness of pets when there is thunder outside or fireworks around the fourth of July. This was like that. The noise and activity were un-nerving because there were many workers outside and then the placing of a safety fence to protect anyone from getting too close and having debris fall on them. The first stage was the removal of the existing roof. Our building has four units in it, each with 1500 square feet in each of two levels.

The roofs were long and a team of eight to ten had their scrapers going to remove the existing roof, the under layment, and of course the thousands of nails holding the roof down. Then the start of the new roof. The under layment came in large heavy roles which were carried to the point they were needed and dropped to the roofs surface. The noise and vibration of these roles hitting the roof surface was like being in a war zone. Once the rolls were where they needed to be, then came the same team nailing down the material. They used nail hammers and it was like machine gun fire. The entire roof had to be covered.

Then came time for the shingles. Again, the packs of shingles had to be placed where they would be placed. The bundles of shingles were very heavy and again when they were carried to the right place they were dropped. Again, the noise of this action was very loud, and the vibrations shook pictures on the wall. I suggested the removal of hearing aids, but this didn't help. She paced the floor and continued to look out the windows because of the concern over the commotion and activity. There were many times when she said there was a need to go out to see if they needed help to get the work done. Not the actual roof construction but the organization of the materials on the ground. I tried to calm the situation by saying there was nothing that could be done outside because the workers were being paid to do what they were doing and any willingness from us to help would only get in their way.

Our routine for three days (only three days that seemed like three months) was disturbed causing a severe state of confusion. Napping wasn't possible. It was too noisy to read. Sitting still didn't work at all because this only happened for 15 minutes at a time. It finally got to me, so we went for long rides to just get away. Interestingly enough, while a state of confusion existed, the result was anger easily over silly things. With short-term memory down to about 3 minutes, the anger did not last.

However, as the confusion persisted with the roof repair, so did the reoccurrence of anger. Finally, the project ended, and the silence was back. Amen. There is always something new. The small things in life are changing and are hard to define. The newest concern is the fact the roofers left a siding trim tool outside of the condo next to the porch. It is difficult to try to explain the entire job wasn't finished and trim around the roof edges still needed to be completed. The tool has been outside for 2 weeks now and every day I'm told it needs to be gone. I told her I have talked to the management company and was told it should be gone early next week. Not soon enough for her. Again, it is the busy activity out of the norm causing this stress. After all, there are 11 buildings needing work to be done.

I may have mentioned this before, but it always surprises me when we come out of anyplace to get into our car, recognizing which car is ours is gone. Often when we get home and I pull into the garage, I am asked "what am I supposed to do now." I will respond with it's time to go into the house. This has never been an issue so far and we just go into the house and settle in until the next adventure begins, which might not be until the next day. I might be asked where we had gone today and I would respond and say something like we went out for lunch at McDonalds and in return she always says, "we did? Where was I? Did I eat?" I tell her you did have lunch and her response is, "I don't remember." I then ask are you hungry? I'm usually told, I'm not sure.

This is not an occasional happening but every

time. Going out to a restaurant to eat is always a fun outing, but when we get there, she never knows what to order nor does she read the menu. If the menu has pictures, she will review this one but always says, "You know what I like. Just order me something". I always know to order finger foods or sandwiches. To put a full restaurant meal in front of her is a waste of money. We might take home a large part of this meal with the intention of eating it later but later never happens. I try to warm it up, but it almost always gets pushed aside, not eaten.

The desire for eating is changing. Breakfast cold cereal with a banana is great for the morning. The noon meal can be a sandwich or other items like chicken nuggets. Dinner is turning out to be a waste of time. The other night I served a favorite chicken pot pie, and this was only ¼ eaten. No matter what I cook, except popcorn or quesadilla's, it often goes without being eaten. Regardless of what I fix, anything other than finger foods, is wasted. Even then she rarely eats much. I know she can't taste or smell anymore. Maybe this is why her eating habits have changed. The exception is <u>any</u> kind of dessert. She has always loved sweet potatoes, so I fixed them often. I also cooked a ham steak the other night and most of it she never ate. I try to offer variety in meal choices and healthy choices, but where are the desserts, I would be asked.

Music has proven to be a calming tool. We have an Alexia which I use to control lights. I will ask it to play Christian music in the morning or Christian songs sung by Elvis Presley. We will sit at the dining room table and sing together. This is a happy time when we do this. Whatever it takes to give the best quality of life possible, I will do it. As we grow older together, it's the small things that work. After all I am 76 years old, and my wife is 82. Activities are limited at our age if for no other reason than ability to get around. The family doctor recently told us my wife is very healthy for her age. We both have some mild issues but basically doing very good.

At this point in the ongoing story of a caregiver, I feel I am just rambling and not offering anything credible to help other caregivers. I know the people around us always ask how I am doing, because they know a caregiver can get burned out after a time of constant care. I tell them I am fine and do not lack for anything. Something that would often help is to have logical adult conversation with another 'normal' adult. When you want to talk about some issue we saw on TV or something that has happened to someone we know, it can be frustrating for me to always have to explain why something happened or to describe an event that caused the issue I was trying to talk about. This comes back to the virtue I have mentioned frequently that all caregivers need, and it can't be said enough, it is patience!

When I try to have a discussion on the phone, it is frustrating for her if I don't use the speaker phone. Then when I do use the speaker phone, it often results in her moving away from the table just to not have to hear the conversation. Perhaps with hearing aids, understanding what is said might be difficult to comprehend if they don't work well. I try to have them adjusted frequently but when the wearer of the hearing aids doesn't grasp how to adjust the noise pick-up, or can't tell another what isn't working right, it's difficult to get the hearing aids to work like they should.

After hearing something someone said, she might feel a response needs to be offered to a point being discussed, which isn't often, her answer can be irrelevant to the question or issue at hand. For example, we could be talking about the COVID-19 virus and the fact the Governor forced the closure of all restaurants to inside dining. Her response could be to paint them green. Being part of a discussion is important and the response was a sincere one and needs to be considered in their mind. Nonetheless, being very satisfied with the response offered, it was time to think about something else. It is important that no response ever received, be mocked or put down because it didn't fit the circumstance. To discourage feedback or conversation is to belittle the person offering it. How wrong would it be to say something like, "that's a stupid thing to say" or "how does that fit into the conversation"? it is always possible to put a positive spin on any comment. No response is as bad as a put down response. You could say "that's an idea to be considered" or "we should think about it".

This is on me and probably the one thing I do miss and that's meaningful conversation. Not a debate but a sharing of thoughts. Oh well, if this is my only concern, I will find a mirror and talk to myself. I don't really do this, but I regularly talk to the Lord and he talks back to me through my spirit. Perhaps this is why God did not give me siblings. As an only child you learn to do things by yourself and learn to listen.

Spring has arrived and our activities are changing. Now the restaurants are opened, and we can go in and have a sit-down meal. All of the distancing photocalls are being followed and we wear a mask into the restaurant until we sit down. Previously I mentioned we bought a golf cart to take rides in the area around our condo. So far this has proven to be the highlight of the day when we take these rides. We go slow and just enjoy the surroundings. There are three small lakes in the subdivision, two of which are accessible to all residents. We ride around them and take in God's splendor in the wild, such as it is in our small area.

I am sure we will both survive as long as the Lord tarries. We both understand the Lord knows the days we have left on this earth and if we keep our eyes on Jesus, the living savior, He will give us a peace to handle the times of the seasons. My only prayer for each of us is to go to heaven in our sleep so we don't have to endure any needless pain. I know this might seem morbid to some, but it is a prayer we share. Keep your eyes on Jesus and not on your situation. I am a caregiver because I choose to be there through sickness and in health, for richer and poorer, till death us do part. This was a promise I made 39 years ago and will stand by it regardless of whether we have 1 day, 1 month, 1 year, or ten more years together.

Growing old together has been a journey over the years and moving a number of times and restarting a life in a new community was a challenge. We have been blessed beyond measure. Through it all, my name might not be remembered, my birthday or her own, when we were married, or what car we are driving every day, but she knows I love her, and she loves me. it doesn't get any better than this. She still loves her hugs and kisses and the big one, holding hands.

Thank you, Lord, for loving us unconditionally and for your many provisions and the years we have left together. Amen

This story is not concluded until the last breath is taken. I thank God for training me to be the right caregiver for my wife and best friend. I also thank God for the wisdom and strength to continue to meet the daily requirements of being a caregiver. Only God knows the plan He has for us and it is meant for good. Romans

8:28 (AMP) in the bible says, "and we know [with great confidence] that God [who is deeply concerned about us] causes all things to work together [as a plan] for good for those who love God, to those who are called according to His plan and purpose." If you believe what the bible says, then you know He is walking with you on this road of being a caregiver.

If you have accepted this role, I pray you have done so by choice, not out of obligation. If you have assumed this role out of obligation, you might feel you have no other choice. There could be many reasons why this might be your situation. It could be because there is no one else to do it, or perhaps the cost for professional care is prohibitive. If the latter is the case, I would suggest you talk to senior care advisors who can lead you to financial help, through Medicaid for example. They can also recommend agencies or groups that can help in providing care with you.

Do not stress over being a caregiver. It is a challenging task to assume, and you must be mentally prepared and equipped to be good at it. No one is perfect and you will make mistakes. It cannot be said enough that every person requiring help to do the things they once could do by themselves is in a unique position. In most cases, it's not where they choose to be but have no choice. You must be there for them and encourage them to accept this fact and to make the best of their life situation. You are not their slave but, in every way, you are their help mate. If you are not received this way by the person needing care, you might need to look at alternatives before you are emotionally destroyed. If you are a caregiver by choice and the process is very challenging, there are many support groups out there where you can at least have an outlet where you can voice your concerns, and perhaps get suggestions on how to make your life better. In the case of working with an Alzheimer's person, there is a chapter of the Alzheimer's Association in most communities or online. The AARP organization also has many resources available where a caregiver can go to find support if needed. You are not alone!

Be strong and never give up if you really care for the person getting care.

EPILOGUE

This book describes the efforts required to care for anyone not completely able to care for themselves any longer, but more specifically what is required, yes required to be a good caregiver. The person needing care could be the result of an accident of any kind, a disabled veteran, someone recovering from an addiction, or in this case suffering from dementia, specifically Alzheimer's disease. Regardless of why care is needed, accepting the role of a caregiver is challenging and can be extremely difficult at times. However, always know you are never alone. If you are blessed and have the Lord to lean on, this is great. I can never completely describe what this relationship has done for me in my role as a caregiver. Hopefully there are family members around you can lean on some. If you attend a church, there are always individuals there usually willing to assist on occasion.

There are also many county and state organizations there to help or at least point you in the right direction to get help when it is needed. In Michigan, we have County Offices on Aging who can provide resources on how to get assistance. If you need an assisted living facility, they can provide guidelines on how to choose a good one. The following web sites are an example of the services they can direct you to:

Assisted Living Residential Care HFA Regulations

https://www.michigan.gov/documents/dhs/

BCAL_PUB_0337_253632_7.pdf

Memory Care Regulationshttps://www.memorycare.com/

memory-care-in-michigan/

Violations -The Department of Licensing &Regulatory Affairs

https://adultfostercare.apps.lara.state.mi.us/

Veterans Affairs offices are always available in every state as are offices on Alzheimer's as well as AARP organizations. Your local phone directory can give you these numbers.

Never feel alone because you are not. The Lord Jesus is there for you if you accept Him as Lord and Savior. He loves us and sacrificed his life for us that we can have hope.